# This col belongs to:

First Edition: 2020

Cardinal

American White Pelican

Bald Eagle

American Flamingo

Allen's Hummingbird

Atlantic Puffin

Mourning Dove

Blue Jay

# Peregrine Falcon

Thick-billed Parrot

Barn Swallow

California Condor

Canada Goose

Common Crane

Common Loon

Blue bird-of-paradise

Red-crested Turaco

American Purple Gallinule

Rainbow Lorikeet

Golden Pheasant

Stork-billed Kingfisher

Great Curassow

Mountain Quail

Spotted Owl

Wild Turkey

Indian Peafowl (Peacock)

American Kestrel

White Stork

Common Raven

Yellow-billed Magpie

Great Blue Heron

Rooster

Hoopoe

Goldcrest

Made in the USA
Columbia, SC
18 March 2022